MARK TOBEY

THE WORLD OF A MARKET

MARK TOBEY

THE WORLD OF A MARKET

University of Washington Press Seattle

*The text of this book was set on the Lintoype in Bodoni Book,
the display type in Bauer Bodoni and ATF Bodoni Open. Haber
Typographers, Inc., New York, and Paul O. Giesey Adcrafters,
Portland, Oregon, were the compositors. The book was printed
by offset lithography at the University of Washington Printing
Plant on Warren's 80 lb. Cameo Brilliant Dull paper. The book
was bound by Lincoln and Allen Company, Portland, Oregon*

DESIGNED BY WILLIAM JAMES

This book is dedicated to those who live in awareness of man's relationship to nature, and who cherish the values of the past as a vital part of the present.

Publisher's Foreword

The association of an artist with one special place—from which he draws apparently inexhaustible inspiration and to which in turn he gives enduring life—is a recurring theme in the history of art. Piranesi in Rome, Hiroshige on the coast of Japan, Van Gogh in Arles—each in his way not only recorded a corner of the world but in so doing created a new world out of his own vision.

In this book, Mark Tobey leads us into the world of Seattle's Public Market, an open-air market near the center of downtown Seattle, overlooking the harbor, which was started in 1907 by a group of local farmers selling their produce from a row of horse-drawn wagons. Frequently threatened with extinction or "modernization" in the name of progress, sanitation, or efficiency, it is stoutly defended by many citizens who feel, as Tobey does, that it is "the heart of Seattle." This is a spot to which Tobey has returned again and again from his travels and sojourns in many countries. In his paintings and sketches, reproduced on the pages that follow, the character—and the characters—of the Market are preserved for all who cherish it.

Acknowledgments

This book had its origin in an exhibition, "Mark Tobey and the Seattle Public Market," held at the Seattle Art Museum in August, 1963. The publisher wishes to thank Dr. Richard Fuller, Mr. Edward Thomas, and Mrs. Betty Bowen, all of the Museum, for their enthusiastic support and assistance, without which the book would not have been possible; and Mr. Earl Fields, the Museum's photographer, who made all the color and black-and-white photographs. The Press also wishes to express its appreciation of the aid and encouragement given by Mr. Otto D. Seligman and Mrs. Marcia Katz of the Otto Seligman Gallery, Seattle; by Dean Joseph L. McCarthy, Dean Solomon Katz, and Professor Victor Steinbrueck of the University of Washington; and by Miss Carolyn Kizer of Seattle. Further thanks are due to the owners of the paintings and sketches for their kind permission to reproduce them; the names of these individuals and institutions will be found in the Catalogue of Plates.

T**HE SKETCHES IN THIS BOOK** show my feeling for the Seattle Market perhaps much better than anything I can say about it. And yet there seems to be a need to speak, today, when drastic changes are going on all around us. Our homes are in the path of freeways; old landmarks, many of a rare beauty, are sacrificed to the urge to get somewhere in a hurry; and when it is all over Progress reigns, queen of hollow streets shadowed by monumental towers left behind by giants to whom the intimacy of living is of no importance. The moon is still far away, but there are forces close by which are ready, with high-sounding words, to dump you out of bed and tear from your sight the colors of joy. And now this unique Market is in danger of being modernized like so much processed cheese.

The Market will always be within me. Established back in 1907 by the farmers themselves—not for the tourist trade, but as a protest against the high prices paid to commission men—it has been for me a refuge, an oasis, a most human growth, the heart and soul of Seattle.

In the twenties, after many years in New York, I walked down this fabulous array of colors and forms. So many things are offered for sale—plants to be replanted; ropes of all kinds; antiques; Norwegian pancakes made by an old sea captain, to be eaten on one of four stools on the sidewalk looking in. I hear the calls to buy—"Hey, you, come over here for the best tomatoes in the Market." Across the street are open shops under long burnt-orange-colored awnings.

The L-shaped Market is alive with all kinds of people, from everywhere, dressed in all kinds of garments, walking under the long shed studded on either side with little cafés, restaurants, and stalls. One man could be from the Black Forest in Germany, and the woman just passing the cucumber stall walks with the stateliness of an Italian princess. Among the men darting here and there is one unsteady on his feet, just dodging the green posts placed at intervals.

Gathered in small groups like islands in the constant stream of people are the men for whom the Market is more than a place of a gathering, almost a home. They live in furnished rooms and rundown hotels, some of them habitués of Skid Road at night and the Market in the day. From the many faces I picked out one man as someone I would like to know. He had looked at me with his friendly eyes—I felt he knew me, so why not speak? "What is your lineage?" But I did not expect the answer I got. "Adam and Eve, just like you, my son."

I ran into my friend again. It was summer, and he was wearing a tropical helmet topped with a small carved wooden duck. His long, yellow-white hair was piled inside. His beard, starting around his eyes, flowed down almost to his waistline. "Come to my studio and let me paint you," I said. "You are an artist, why don't you paint your impression?" I made no further comment. He was a king of the Market.

For me every day in the Market was a fiesta. But, alas, wars came; the old men I had learned to know died; more and more stalls were empty; the Japanese were sent away. Mrs. Morgan, who ran a flower stand, said, "Mr. Tobey, the Market ist deadt!" The years dissolve, and I return to visit the Market. A few old friends remain—the brothers of the fish stall, but the interesting sign above their heads has been stolen. The chairs that ascended the incline directly below them, upon which tired shoppers used to rest, have been torn out. But the main part of the Market is still active, still varied, exciting, and terribly important in the welter of overindustrialization. There is the same magic as night approaches: the sounds fade; there is an extra rustle everywhere; prices drop; the garbage pickers come bending and sorting; the cars leave the street which reflects the dying sun. The windows are all that remain of light as the sun sets over the Olympics. A few isolated figures appear and disappear, and then the Market is quiet, awaiting another day.

January, 1964
Basle

Catalogue of Plates

In dimensions height precedes width.

1 FARMERS' MARKET, tempera, 1941, 19⅝" x 15⅝", Seattle Art Museum, Eugene Fuller Memorial Collection

2 POINT FIVE—VERTICAL, tempera, 1943, 28½" x 19⅛", Seattle Art Museum

3 MARKET PLACE, tempera, 1944, 11¾" x 7½", Mr. and Mrs. David Lewis, Seattle

4 RUMMAGE, tempera, 1941, 38⅜" x 25⅞", Seattle Art Museum, Eugene Fuller Memorial Collection

5 E PLURIBUS UNUM, tempera, 1942, 19¾" x 27¼", Seattle Art Museum, gift of the late Mrs. Thomas D. Stimson

6 Tempera, 1943, 8¼" x 5½", Mr. and Mrs. Arthur G. Barnett, Bainbridge Island, Washington

7 TIME OFF, oil, 1941, 19⅝" x 15½", Seattle Art Museum, Eugene Fuller Memorial Collection

8 MARKET, tempera, 1945, 23¼" x 21⅜", Dr. and Mrs. Clinton R. Vitous, Seattle

9 Tempera, 1941, 8½" x 5⅝", Mr. and Mrs. David E. Wyman, Seattle

10 Tempera, 1941, 8⅝" x 5⅝", Mrs. William R. McMillan, Seattle

11 Tempera, 1940, 8¾" x 6", Mr. and Mrs. Cedric M. Wardall, Seattle

12 Tempera, 1940, 8⅝" x 5¾", Mr. and Mrs. Eli Rashkov, Seattle

13 Tempera, no date, 6¾" x 4¾", Mr. and Mrs. Eli Rashkov, Seattle

14 Tempera, 1939, 8⅝" x 5⅝", the late Mrs. Thomas D. Stimson, Seattle

15 Tempera, 1939, 8⅝" x 5⅝", the late Mrs. Thomas D. Stimson, Seattle

16 Tempera, no date, ca. 8⅝" x 5⅝", the late Mrs. Thomas D. Stimson, Seattle

17 Tempera, 1942, 8⅝" x 5⅝", Mr. and Mrs. Eli Rashkov, Seattle

18 Tempera, 1941, 8¾" x 5¾", the late Mrs. Thomas D. Stimson, Seattle

19 Tempera, 1941, ca. 8⅝" x 5⅝", the late Mrs. Thomas D. Stimson, Seattle

20 Tempera, 1940, 8⅝" x 5⅝", Mr. and Mrs. Prescott Oakes, Seattle

21 Tempera, 1941, 8¾" x 5⅝", Mrs. William R. McMillan, Seattle

22 Tempera, 1939, 8⅝" x 5⅝", the late Mrs. Thomas D. Stimson, Seattle

23 Tempera, 1940, 8½" x 5⅝", Dr. and Mrs. George C. Marshall, Seattle

24 Tempera, 1939, 8⅝" x 5⅝", the late Mrs. Thomas D. Stimson, Seattle

25 Tempera, no date, 8⅝" x 5⅝", Mrs. Robert D. McAusland, Seattle

26 Tempera, 1940, 5¹¹⁄₁₆" x 7¾", Dr. Audrey Holliday, Seattle

27 Tempera, 1940, 8½" x 5½", Mr. and Mrs. David E. Wyman, Seattle

28 Tempera, 1941, ca. 8⅝" x 5⅝", Seattle Art Museum, Eugene Fuller Memorial Collection

29 Tempera, 1941, ca. 8⅝" x 5⅝", Seattle Art Museum, Eugene Fuller Memorial Collection

30 Tempera, 1940, 8½" x 5½", Mr. and Mrs. David E. Wyman, Seattle

31 Tempera, 1942, 8⅝" x 5⅝", Dr. and Mrs. Henry R. Richards, Seattle

32 Tempera, 1941, 8⅝" x 5¾", Captain and Mrs. John H. Bowen, Seattle

33 Tempera, 1941, 8⅝" x 5⅝", the late Mrs. Thomas D. Stimson, Seattle

34 Tempera, 1942, ca. 8⅝" x 5⅝", Otto Seligman Gallery, Seattle

35 Tempera, 1941, ca. 8⅝" x 5⅝", Seattle Art Museum, Eugene Fuller Memorial Collection

36 Tempera, 1942, 8⅝" x 5¾", Mr. and Mrs. Joseph E. Gandy, Seattle

37 Tempera, 1942, 8¾" x 5¾", Dr. and Mrs. Henry M. Richards, Seattle

38 Tempera, 1941, ca. 8⅝" x 5⅝", Seattle Art Museum, Eugene Fuller Memorial Collection

39 Tempera, 1941, 12½" x 20", Mr. and Mrs. Prentice Bloedel, Bainbridge Island, Washington

40 Tempera, 1940, 8⅝" x 5⅝", Mr. and Mrs. Prescott Oakes, Seattle

41 Tempera, 1941, 8⅝" x 5⅝", the late Mrs. Thomas D. Stimson, Seattle

42 Tempera, 1941, 8⅝" x 5⅝", the late Mrs. Thomas D. Stimson, Seattle

43 Brown ink, 1939, 8" x 5⅝", Mr. and Mrs. Ralph W. Nicholson, Seattle

44 Brown ink, 1939, ca. 8⅝" x 5⅝", Mr. and Mrs. Ralph W. Nicholson, Seattle

45 Brown ink, 1941, ca. 8⅝" x 5⅝", Mr. Ed Raskov, Seattle

46 Brown ink, 1941, ca. 8⅝" x 5⅝", Otto Seligman Gallery, Seattle

47 Brown ink, 1941, ca. 8⅝" x 5⅝", Otto Seligman Gallery, Seattle

48 Brown ink, 1941, ca. 8⅝" x 5⅝", Mr. Ed Raskov, Seattle

49 Brown ink, 1941, ca. 8⅝" x 5⅝", Otto Seligman Gallery, Seattle

50 Brown ink, 1941, ca. 8⅝" x 5⅝", Otto Seligman Gallery, Seattle

51 Brown ink, 1941, ca. 8⅝" x 5⅝", Mr. Ed Raskov, Seattle

52 Brown ink, 1941, ca. 8⅝" x 5⅝", Mr. Ed Raskov, Seattle

53 Black ink, 1941, 8⅝" x 5⅝", Otto Seligman Gallery, Seattle

54 Brown ink, no date, ca. 8⅝" x 5⅝", Mr. and Mrs. Ralph W. Nicholson, Seattle

55 Black ink, 1941, 8⅝" x 5⅝", Otto Seligman Gallery, Seattle

56 Brown ink, 1941, ca. 8⅝" x 5⅝", Otto Seligman Gallery, Seattle

57 Brown ink, 1941, ca. 8⅝" x 5⅝", Mr. Ed Raskov, Seattle

58 Brown ink, 1941, ca. 8⅝" x 5⅝", Mr. Ed Raskov, Seattle

59 Black ink, 1941, ca. 8⅝" x 5⅝", Otto Seligman Gallery, Seattle

60 Brown ink, 1941, ca. 8⅝" x 5⅝", Mr. Ed Raskov, Seattle

61 Black ink, no date, ca. 8⅝" x 5⅝", Mr. and Mrs. Ralph W. Nicholson, Seattle

62 Black ink, 1941, 8⅝" x 5⅝", Otto Seligman Gallery, Seattle

63 Black ink, no date, ca. 8⅝" x 5⅝", Mr. and Mrs. Ralph W. Nicholson, Seattle

64 Brown ink, 1941, ca. 8⅝" x 5⅝", Mr. Ed Raskov, Seattle

MARK TOBEY

THE WORLD OF A MARKET

3

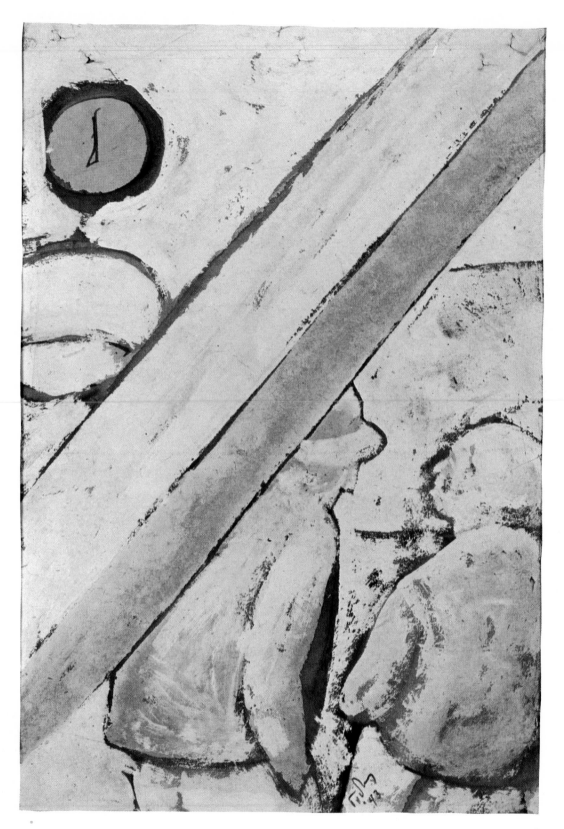

6

8

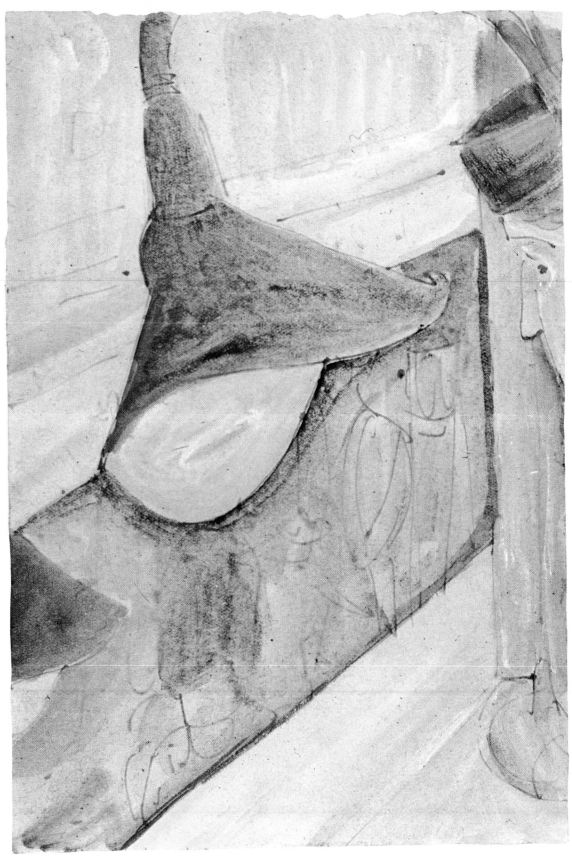

12

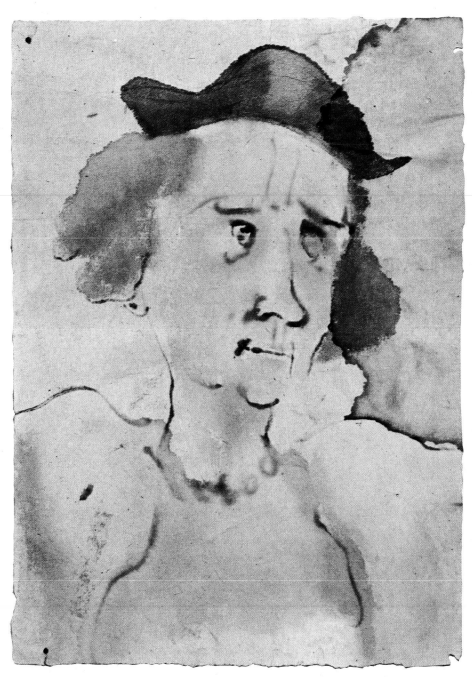

13

14

16

17

21

23

24

25

26

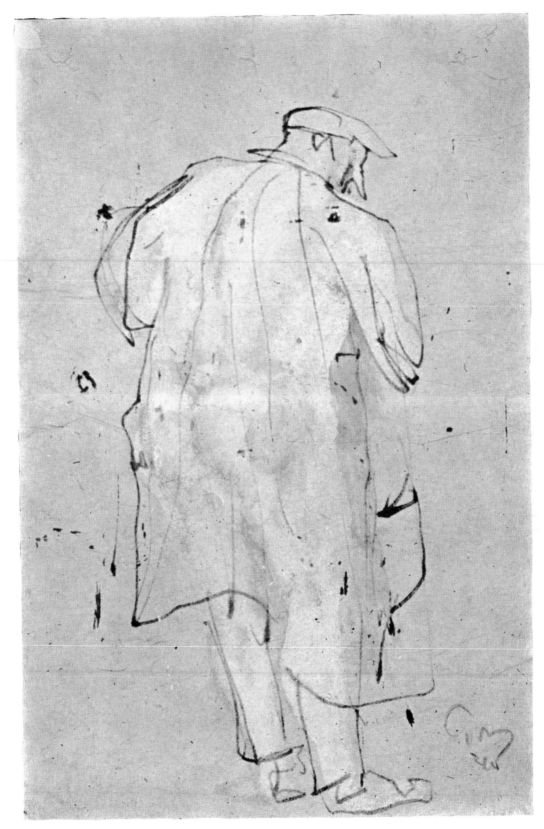

27

28

33

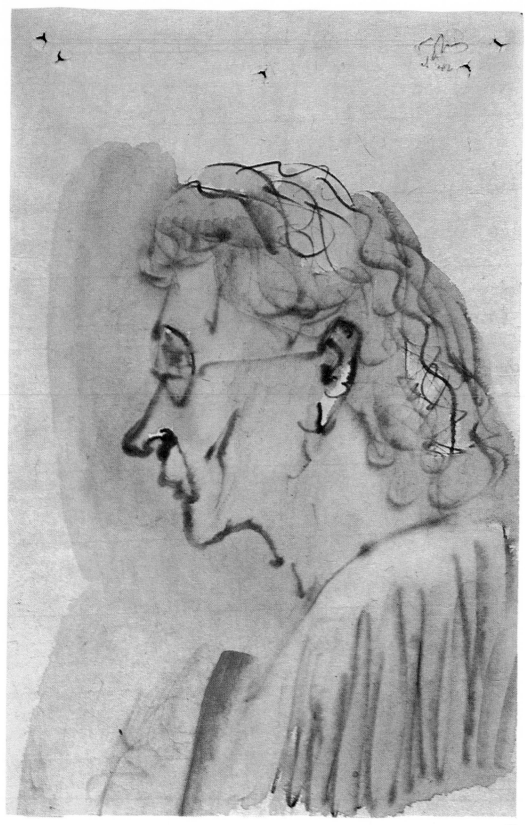

34

35

36

39

58

60